Original title:
The Meaning of Life? Still Decoding

Copyright © 2025 Creative Arts Management OÜ
All rights reserved.

Author: Beckett Sinclair
ISBN HARDBACK: 978-1-80566-217-4
ISBN PAPERBACK: 978-1-80566-512-0

Threads of Infinity

Life's a thread, that's tangled tight,
We pull and tug, with all our might.
But as we sew our hopes and dreams,
We find out life is full of seams.

Laughing at puzzles, we just can't solve,
The bobbin's empty, where's the resolve?
A needle's prick brings wisdom's spark,
In the fabric of life, we make our mark.

Celestial Puzzles

Stars are winking, do they know?
Are they amused by our life's show?
We gaze and wonder, looking up,
While spilling coffee in our cup.

Constellations, a wild game,
Each star's a player, wild and tame.
We're just players on this board,
Dodging troubles, never bored.

Echoes of Tomorrow

What whispers back from future's shore?
Do echoes laugh or just implore?
We throw our hopes like paper planes,
With dreams that catch the winds of rains.

Tomorrow giggles, 'What's your plan?'
A recipe made without a pan.
We trip and stumble, yet we stand,
With laughter, life's a witty hand.

The Language of Stars

Words of wisdom, penned in night,
Stars converse in beams of light.
Catching phrases on the breeze,
Translation found in tiny leaves.

Do they joke about our plight?
With cosmic smirks, they shine so bright.
As we decode this comic book,
Guided by starlight's sly look.

The Fabric of our Fate

Threads weave in all directions,
Stitching dreams of odd collections.
A sock lost here, a shoe misplaced,
We laugh aloud at life's wild chase.

Patterns form in such strange ways,
A life of puzzles, quirky plays.
With tangled yarn and humor bright,
We find our path in threads of light.

Write Your Own Odyssey

Grab a pen, just take some risks,
Plot twists and turns, add some zips.
Monsters lurking? Oh, what fun!
Just write it down, let chaos run.

A hero's journey? Not quite right,
Let's change the script, invite a kite.
With laughter loud, we set the tone,
Creating tales that are our own.

Eclipses of Understanding

When wisdom hides, what a sight!
Like a moon blocking out the light.
We giggle at things we can't explain,
A circus of thoughts inside our brain.

Oh, knowledge slips and tumbles down,
A silly dance, we all clown around.
Through goofy grins and distant stares,
We journey on, ignoring our cares.

The Soundtrack of Silence

In quiet moments, whispers play,
A symphony of thoughts gone astray.
Can you hear the crickets hum?
Or is it just my stomach's drum?

While pondering life, a dog barks loud,
And laughter erupts in the bustling crowd.
So here we stand, a joyful band,
Creating tunes, hand in hand.

The Language of Souls

In whispers of dreams, we chat with the stars,
As socks disappear, we debate from afar.
Is it just a riddle or the universe's prank?
With giggles and snacks, we ponder and thank.

Do fish have thoughts or just swim in a daze?
And do clouds take naps while they drift through our gaze?
If life's just a game, who's keeping the score?
Let's laugh at the chaos, and then ask for more!

Fragments of Light

In the kitchen we dance, where the toast always burns,
While questioning fate, as the kettle still churns.
We chase after shadows, with a broom in our hand,
Trying to catch wisdom like grains of fine sand.

A cat has its secrets, it winks with a grin,
As if in a game where the rules are all thin.
With friends and some laughter, we float down the stream,

In search of the answers, or just a good meme.

Navigating the Unknown

With maps made of jelly and compasses spun,
We tumble through questions, looking for fun.
Is that a wise sage, or just a talking tree?
We giggle at nonsense, so wild and so free.

In a world made of jigsaw, each piece is a clue,
With riddles on napkins, and puzzle glue too.
We spin on our chairs, as ideas take flight,
Chasing wild thoughts into the depths of the night.

Threads of Purpose

With yarn made of laughter, we weave through the day,
Unraveling mysteries in a whimsical way.
Do ducks have a meaning, or just quack for the fun?
We ponder these questions 'til the setting sun.

In the garden of chaos, we plant seeds of cheer,
Hoping to harvest a harvest of beer.
With jokes and reminders, we lighten the load,
As we dance through the weeds, on this curious road.

The Art of Living

In a world of tasks and duties,
I juggle cats and eat some cuties.
Sipping coffee like a pro,
Life's a circus, don't you know?

I tried to dance but tripped on air,
Stole the spotlight with a glare.
With every blunder, I just grin,
Life's a game, let's begin!

Dreams Beyond the Horizon

I dreamt a dream of flying high,
On a pizza slice, oh my oh my!
The cheese was thick, the crust divine,
I asked the clouds for a glass of wine.

But then I fell into a bread bowl,
With salad greens that took a stroll.
Do dreams mean I'm losing it fast?
Or am I just having a delicious blast?

Fleeting Seconds

Seconds tick like cheeky mice,
They scamper by with quite the spice.
I chase them down, they giggle loud,
While I'm just here, lost in a crowd.

A minute here, a minute there,
Sometimes I'm still, like a dying hare.
But who needs time? Let's grab a snack,
Or hug a tree, then head back!

Timeless Questions

Why is cheese round, and pizza square?
Does the clock really even care?
I asked a sock, it just replied,
'Life's a mystery, let's take a ride!'

With questions flying like confetti,
Answers run off, so unsteady.
I'll ponder deep while eating cake,
Life's too short for all the heartache!

The Spectrum of Seeking

I seek the truth with purple shades,
In a music shop, where logic fades.
Guitars sing songs of cosmic cheer,
While I just nod and sip my beer.

A rainbow's end holds pots of gold,
But what's the worth? It's getting old!
Let's flip a coin and call it a day,
Pursuing fun, come what may!

Flickers of Clarity

In the fridge lies an old pie,
Its mystery will never die.
I ponder while I take a bite,
Is this dessert or a fright?

I ask the stars, they just giggle,
With each twinkle, they make me wiggle.
Questions dance like shadows do,
As I sip my old green brew.

A rubber duck floats by my thoughts,
In hazy dreams, a sailor mocks.
Life's puzzle pieces seldom fit,
But here I am, still throwing fits.

Laughter rings in every quest,
In chaos, there's a jest.
Seeking sense in jumbled days,
While joking through this funky maze.

Fragile Fortunes

A dollar bill, torn and tattered,
In my pocket, dreams are scattered.
I hold it close, as if it's fate,
While staring at my empty plate.

Fortune cookies, cracked and broken,
Read too much into each token.
Sit back, relax, and tell a tale,
Of how I chased a dancing snail.

On busy streets, I trip and fall,
Searching for wisdom, or just a call.
With every stumble, lessons bloom,
In the chaos, there's room for room.

The riches aren't in shiny gold,
But in laughter, brisk and bold.
So grab your pie and join the spree,
In fragile fortunes, be truly free!

Journeys in the Mind's Eye

I take a ride on my wild brain,
Dodging thoughts that look like rain.
Chasing dreams down twisted lanes,
While juggling cats and popcorn grains.

A sandwich talks, it's quite a sight,
Debating life from day to night.
A hungry bug with plans so grand,
Says paper plates should rule the land.

With clowns and hats made from old socks,
Life's puzzles unfold like paradox.
Mismatched shoes lead the way,
To a circus where the wild owls play.

Here and there, the laughter flows,
In dreams where anything goes.
Each whimsy holds a spark so bright,
In these journeys, we take flight.

Facets of Forever

A shiny coin spins 'twixt my fingers,
As wisdom's laughter suddenly lingers.
Heads or tails, the question's there,
Oh, how I wish life had a spare!

In the corner, a dancing chair,
It wiggles and twists, without a care.
I join the fun and twirl about,
In these moments, I can't doubt.

Books of riddles though dusty sit,
Every page, a cheeky bit.
The soles of my shoes, worn and old,
Tread paths where strange tales unfold.

Forever's just a playful jest,
Filled with giggles and tongue-in-cheek tests.
So here I stand, with smiles applied,
In facets of forever, we won't hide.

Readings in the Dark

We ponder with a flashlight, so bright,
What's it all about? We laugh in the night.
Is it cake or a riddle, we can't quite tell,
Life's menu is puzzling, like a crab in a shell.

We flip through the pages of humor and lore,
Searching for answers behind every door.
Yet every time we peek, we just see more snacks,
Philosophy's a buffet; just don't eat the wax!

Amid those deep thoughts, we giggle and snort,
Debating the merits of a well-cooked tort!
Laughter erupts as we ponder the question,
Do ducks have a purpose, or are they just jesters?

In our scribbles and sketches, we find silly cues,
Each line a new giggle, or a clever excuse.
We call out for wisdom, like kids at a fair,
But it's just more balloons drifting up in the air.

The Circle of Inquiry

In a cozy little circle, we sit with delight,
With questions like popcorn, taking flight!
"Why is the sky blue?" we ask with a grin,
As a sage munches chips and dives right in.

"Can cats truly fly?" we muse with a laugh,
Imagining felines with wings, what a gaffe!
In this quest for the truth, the giggles come fast,
We find wisdom in jest, and joy unsurpassed.

Our thoughts swirl like candy on a merry-go-round,
Each joke a new layer of wisdom profound.
"Is life just a sitcom?" we joke and we jest,
Trying to decode this unending test.

With each silly theory, we flex and we bend,
Like pretzels in thought, on the verge of a trend.
So we sip our sweet drinks to fuel this quest,
For answers like cookies are better when blessed.

Unveiling Layered Truths

In a world made of layers, like cake and good cheer,
We slice through the frosting, devouring our fear.
Are we but the sprinkles, sweet on the top?
Or serious layers that make laughter stop?

As they peel back the onion, they start to cry,
But we cheer them up with a pie in the sky!
With each layer we shed, we giggle and beam,
Life's more of a riddle, or so it would seem.

We question the cosmos over cups of hot tea,
Do fish have regrets? Is a frog truly free?
Every query unfolds like a joke in the mirror,
The deeper we search, the funnier they appear!

With winks at the stars, we dance through the night,
Chasing those truths that give giggles more height.
Perhaps all we find is a joke to retell,
In this game of layers, we laugh, and we dwell.

Breath of Existence

I woke up this morning, what a surprise,
Did the universe giggle? I heard no cries.
Coffee's my compass, it leads me ahead,
Without it, I promise, I'd still be in bed.

The cat at my feet gives a satisfied yawn,
Is he plotting my fate? I feel strangely drawn.
Life's a big puzzle with pieces gone wild,
I laugh at my chaos, for I'm still a child.

The Landscape of Longing

A wish on a star, but it fell in the soup,
I'd fish it out quick, if I could find a scoop.
Life's like my fridge, half-empty, half-full,
The light's always flickering, but hey, it's still cool.

In gardens of dreams where the weeds intertwine,
I chase after butterflies, sipping on wine.
Each sip's a sweet ponder, a thought that's unclear,
But I dance on the lawn, without any fear.

Dreams Shattered and Whole

My plans are like glass, it's a risky ballet,
I trip on my hopes like they're shoes gone astray.
The ladder to wisdom, it wobbles and shakes,
Yet laughter is glue for the life that it makes.

I tried to catch dreams, but they slipped through my hands,
Like fish in a stream, or those weird rubber bands.
Yet here I am grinning, missteps and all,
Finding joy in the stumbles, without fear of the fall.

Dances with Ambiguity

Twist, twirl, and spin in this life's weird ballet,
With hiccups and giggles, we dance all the way.
The music is odd, like a cat on the keys,
But who needs a plan when you've got subtle tease?

A friend once said wisdom is baked in a pie,
But the crust gets too soggy when baked in a lie.
So let's savor a slice of uncertainty's cake,
With a cherry on top, here's to fun we can make!

Labyrinth of Longing

In a maze of dreams we wander around,
Chasing bits of joy that can't be found.
We trip on thoughts that make us trip,
Who knew life's treasures could be a quip?

With cupcakes for wisdom and coffee for clues,
We juggle our hopes while wearing mismatched shoes.
An onion of purpose with layers so odd,
Peeling back laughter, hoping to nod.

Transient Tales

Once I met a sage who wore a bright hat,
He said life's like juggling—this and that!
With each toss of fate, avoid all the mess,
But honestly, I must confess...

We're all just like socks—lost in the wash,
Hoping to pair up, oh what a posh!
Between laughs and mishaps, we dance on the line,
In this circus of chaos, isn't it fine?

Navigating Through Nebulae

In a rocket of whimsy, we float through the dark,
Counting the wishes that missed their mark.
With meteors of feelings and comets of fun,
Our GPS says 'turn left'—who knows where we run?

Stars wink and giggle, they tease and they swirl,
What's out there in space? A universe twirl!
With each twist and turn, we sip on the stars,
Claiming our place amongst Venus and Mars.

Beneath the Surface of Silence

In whispers of quiet, where chuckles reside,
Lurk thoughts of grandeur, and giggles collide.
With each awkward pause, the humor will grow,
Who knew that silence could steal the show?

Like cats in a box, we ponder the void,
What means something to the absurdly annoyed?
In the still of the night, we trip over jest,
Searching for answers in a cosmic quest.

Whispered Wonders

In a world where socks do stray,
I ponder questions every day.
Is it fate or just a prank,
Why do they go? My mind's a blank.

Coffee spills, the toast that's burnt,
Life teaches lessons, I discerned.
With every laugh and every blunder,
I seek the truth beneath the thunder.

Patterns of Perception

The puzzles hide in kitchen drawers,
Among the spatulas and old floors.
A riddle wrapped in bacon grease,
What can I say? I seek release.

Every friend a quirky guide,
With jokes that twist, they never hide.
In chaos blooms the sweetest jest,
Life's a riddle, a playful quest.

The Quest for Understanding

I sought the truth in a cereal box,
Found riddles shaped like silly clocks.
An apple core with wisdom's weight,
Is the fridge a sage? Oh, contemplate!

A banana peel slips, I shout,
The quirky path I'm on, no doubt.
With giggles loud and giggles bright,
I chase answers in the moonlight.

Celestial Threads

Stars gossip tales of cupcakes and fun,
While wise old moons play hide-and-run.
A cosmic dance of salad greens,
What's next, a laugh? We'll join the scenes!

The universe winks, a secret shared,
In every giggle, we're unprepared.
From planets soft to comets bold,
Life's a circus, a tale retold!

The Alchemy of Awareness

In a world full of whys,
We search for the clues,
Chasing echoes of laughter,
While dodging the blues.

Coffee stains on the floor,
Maps that lead us astray,
Each sip is a riddle,
That somehow got away.

Between hiccups and sighs,
We dance like a fool,
Finding gold in the nonsense,
While breaking the rule.

So let's toast to the jest,
With a wink and a smile,
For in chaos and bliss,
We're all on the dial.

Words Unspoken

Tickling thoughts in my brain,
Silent giggles take flight,
Whispers lost in the din,
Shy shadows of light.

In a world full of chatter,
Tongues twist and they twirl,
But laughter needs no voice,
It's a universal pearl.

Muffled messages sneak,
Like ninjas in the night,
Trying hard to convince,
That wrongs can feel right.

So here's to the pauses,
That smear life with fun,
Some truths are quite silly,
Yet merrily spun.

Ciphers of the Heart

Love's a puzzle we play,
With pieces askew,
Curly cues in the margin,
Or a cat's meow, too.

Hold my hand and let's leap,
Through whispers and sighs,
Unlocking the secrets,
With our goofy tries.

This love code we scribble,
Through laughter and cheer,
Turns frowns into chuckles,
When you are near.

So let's break out the crayons,
And color outside,
Life's a game of charades,
With you as my guide.

Beyond the Horizons of Time

Time's a jester on wheels,
Spinning tales and some tricks,
While we're hopping through moments,
Like a bag of magic sticks.

Each tick is a giggle,
Each tock wears a grin,
We're juggling our hours,
While the clock pulls us in.

So sail with the waves,
Where the past meets the now,
With surprises around,
We'll laugh and allow.

Let's flip through the pages,
Of lessons we've learned,
In this humor-filled journey,
Our spirits have turned.

Mosaic of Moments

Tiny pieces fit so snug,
Life's craziest puzzle, what a tug.
I lost the corner with a grin,
Turns out, it's where the fun begins.

Coffee spills and socks that stray,
Counting laughs at the end of the day.
We dance through chaos like a pro,
Who knew confusion could steal the show?

Each snicker counts, each giggle gleams,
Finding joy in silly dreams.
Laughter's echo, a guiding light,
In this wild game, we just might take flight.

So here's to moments, odd as they seem,
Stitching life together, a quirky theme.
We're all just dots in a grand parade,
And in this mess, pure joy's displayed.

Shadows of Purpose

Caught between the couch and fate,
Decisions made after lunch at eight.
Chasing goals down hallways wide,
While snacks become my trusty guide.

In shadows lurk the whims we choose,
Pondering paths that all amuse.
Do I take the road less strolled?
Or stick to Netflix, blissfully rolled?

The search for meaning's like my cat,
Sleeping soundly, where's my hat?
Purpose pops up like a giant troll,
Saying, 'Hey, watch out for that hole!'

With every stumble and joyful sigh,
I paint my canvas, oh me, oh my!
For in the shadows, truths collide,
And laughter's echo is my proud guide.

Chasing Clarity

Running after answers, 'What's the trick?'
Lost in a maze, I take my pick.
A map of riddles made of cheese,
Each bite brings wisdom, life's just a tease.

Sudden insights hit like rain,
Wait, what did I just explain?
In flashes bright, my thoughts collide,
Then disappear, like time's last ride.

Scribbling notes with crayons bright,
A child's view gives me delight.
Life's strange puzzle, a jokester's dream,
I laugh aloud—what's my theme?

So here I am, with sticky notes,
Tripping through life in silly boats.
Chasing clarity like a playful sprite,
And in this chase, I just might take flight.

Tides of Thought

Waves of musings crash on shore,
Thoughts flip-flop, who could ask for more?
They pull away, then rush right back,
Like ocean whispers, they leave a track.

Riding currents, lost at sea,
Confused with purpose, oh, what a spree!
Each bob and weave brings smiles anew,
Life's an ocean, invite the crew!

Floating on dreams, I catch the breeze,
A jellyfish dance with utmost ease.
The tide shifts swiftly; I sway along,
In the splashy chaos, I find my song.

So let the waves wash over me,
A splash of laughter, wild and free.
Through these tides, I'll take a chance,
In every ripple, there's a lively dance.

Unraveling Time's Tapestry

Once I asked a turtle slow,
"What's your secret? Let me know!"
He winked and smiled, just took a nap,
"Life's a tale, don't need a map!"

I pondered hard, I scratched my head,
Through fields of thoughts, my mind was led.
A squirrel danced, he joined the spree,
"Life's a puzzle; just be free!"

The flowers whispered, bees did hum,
Why so serious? Let's just have fun!
A cloud shaped like a silly hat,
"Get moving, friend! Life's just that!"

So if you find a riddle weird,
Just laugh it off, don't be afeared.
For time's a joke, a playful thing,
Just dance along, and hear it sing!

The Pursuit of Essence

In search of crumbs of wisdom wide,
I tripped and fell, but that's my ride.
A donut smiled, said, "What a treat!"
"Life's a hole, so take a seat!"

A cat named Whiskers held a sign,
"Chase the fish, oh, it's divine!"
With paws in air, it showed the way,
To find joy in the oddest play.

A jester danced beneath the moon,
"Hey there, buddy! Join the tune!"
With every skip, life's charms appeared,
A comic strip of laughs endeared.

So leap and laugh, embrace the quest,
For in the jest, we find our best.
The essence shines in goofy ways,
In every chuckle, life's bouquets!

Echoes of Infinity

In a land where echoes fade,
I met a frog who croaked and played.
"What's the score in life's grand game?"
"Just hop along, don't feel the shame!"

A wise old owl perched on a tree,
"Can you decipher your folly?"
With a wink and a flappy cheer,
"Life's a riddle—just persevere!"

The stars above began to wink,
"Connect the dots; don't let it stink!"
With every giggle and silly face,
Infinity's just a funny place.

So if you find a maze of thought,
Remember joy is what you sought.
In echoes loud, or whispers low,
Life's a stage, so give a show!

Searching for Forgotten Truths

With a hat of lamps and shoes of foam,
I ventured out, but felt like home.
A dog declared, "Let's sniff it out!"
"The truth is lost!" he barked with clout.

I wandered lanes, the street was wide,
A sign said, "Truth is on this ride!"
I jumped aboard a quirky bus,
"Next stop, wisdom! Hop on, trust!"

A disco ball spun truth around,
With every sparkle, laughter found.
A chicken danced upon the floor,
"Life's a joke, says cluck, y'all want more?"

So chase the fun, not just the facts,
For wisdom hides in laughter's pacts.
Forget the rules and just embrace,
The silly dance—that's the true grace!

Eternal Questions

Why do we stare at the stars?
Are they just bright, distant cars?
Sometimes they wink, sometimes they blink,
Are they asking us to think?

Is there a manual we just missed?
Lost amongst dreams and cosmic trysts?
Life's a game, or so it seems,
Yet we search for answers in our dreams.

Why do socks vanish in the wash?
Can missing keys cause such a posh?
Is the cat secretly in charge?
With nine lives, does he loom large?

Oh, the joy of pondering it all,
Like standing too close to a wall.
We laugh as we grill the great unknown,
With each jest, a wisdom we're shown.

Fragments of Existence

Jigsaw pieces, scattered wide,
Hiding secrets we can't bide.
Laughter echoes in our quest,
While we're searching for the best.

Why do we trip on our own feet?
Life's a dance, or just a beat?
The cake of wisdom's full of crumbs,
Yet we munch as confusion comes.

Cookies crumbled, flavors blend,
Searching for the perfect friend.
Is the universe a giant joke?
With a punchline we barely spoke?

With each giggle, we find our way,
Through the madness of the day.
Life's a riddle wrapped in cheer,
We decode it all with lots of beer.

Whispers of the Cosmos

Stars chatting like gossip queens,
Sharing tales of celestial means.
Do they giggle about our plight?
Or are they lost in endless night?

Galaxies swirl in cosmic dance,
Do they plot and play, given a chance?
With telescopes, we try to see,
Yet miss the joys of being free.

Are black holes just a lunch break?
Waiting for light to take a shake?
We ponder as we sip our tea,
Unraveling what it could be.

In this universe of quirky fun,
With paradoxes on the run.
We find delight in every jest,
As we ponder life's crazy quest.

Unraveling Existence

Like puzzles scattered on the floor,
Each piece holds secrets, myths, and lore.
Laughter bubbles as we explore,
The puzzle's missing, but we want more.

Are we just bits in a grand machine?
Riding waves of absurd, unseen?
Life's absurdity, a tasty bite,
More hilarious than a moth in flight.

Why do we chase a wayward dream?
In our mind, does reality scream?
Each moment's laugh is all we own,
Like a throne made from sticks and stone.

So let's toast to whims of fate,
With goofy smiles that never abate.
In unraveling this wacky show,
Laughter's the best path we know.

Universe in a Grain of Sand

A grain of sand, a tiny speck,
Holds galaxies from neck to neck.
Asteroids dance with grains of glee,
While the sun plans its next big spree.

Cosmic jokes in a beach chair's sway,
Where seagulls ponder their buffet.
Why is the ocean blue, I wonder?
Maybe it's hiding from the thunder!

Stars wink from their sandy throne,
While crabs plot ways to chill alone.
The tide rolls in, the tide rolls out,
Is life just a game we laugh about?

So gather 'round with your grainy friend,
In this vast universe, let's pretend.
With laughter and sand between our toes,
Let's toast to life, wherever it goes!

The Poetry of Being

In the garden, flowers chat and gossip,
'Hey, did you see that bug with the red hop?'
Leaves debate on who's the best tree,
But none can agree; it's a giddy spree!

Sunshine tickles the grass in delight,
While weeds dance around, oh what a sight!
The breeze sneezes, sending petals to flee,
Who knew existence could be so free?

Chickens cluck wisdom beneath their shells,
In rhymes and riddles, their secret spells.
Life's little quirks make them giggle and squawk,
Silly, just like a heart's sweet talk!

So savor each moment, quirks and all,
For in this playground, we learn to stand tall.
With laughter as sweet as the honeyed bee,
The poetry of being brings us glee!

Soul Seeds

Soul seeds scattered by the wind,
Sprouting ideas where joy begins.
Some land in laughter, some in tears,
All sprouting stories that tickle your fears.

In a garden of thoughts, what do we grow?
Comedic antics in a joyful show.
A wiggle, a giggle, a tumble and fall,
Even the plants are having a ball!

Rooted in whimsy, tangled with fate,
Flowering thoughts on a playful plate.
The sun winks down, sharing its light,
Encouraging growth in the goofy night.

So water those seeds with laughter and cheer,
Let them blossom throughout the year.
In this soul garden, we're free to roam,
Finding our way in this whimsical home!

Kaleidoscope of Now

Twist the lens and what do you see?
Colors of chaos in a reverie.
Time's a jester, playing hide-and-seek,
As we chase rainbows, cheek to cheek.

Moments dissolve like a melted treat,
Giggling at life's sugary feat.
Yesterday's frown, tomorrow's surprise,
A kaleidoscope whirls, opens our eyes.

Each chuckle echoes, a blissful sound,
Looping through sweetness that's all around.
With each twist of fate, we learn to flow,
This dance of life is a splendid show!

So embrace the lens, it's quite a ride,
Through colors and laughter, let's slide.
In this kaleidoscope, let's take our bow,
For each twist reveals the magic of now!

Imagining Infinity

What's up with all the stars,
Are they just bright little cars?
Zooming through the cosmic night,
With a wink, they take their flight.

Time to ponder the great unknown,
Is it a circus or just a drone?
Do we laugh or cry in space,
While juggling thoughts in a dizzy race?

Questions swirl like cotton candy,
Sweet and sticky, kinda dandy.
Do we chase or do we rest?
In this riddle, we're all guests.

Let's giggle at this cosmic plight,
As we chase our dreams in flight.
Living life, a silly ride,
Through imagination we decide.

Cycles of Connection

Round and round, we come and go,
Like a yo-yo in a freaky show.
Tangled up in life's ballet,
Connecting dots in a quirky way.

Friends are stars on this spinning wheel,
They shine, they twinkle, they make us feel.
But sometimes they act a silly fool,
Forget the recipe but still play cool.

Life's a merry-go-round of fate,
Where laughter holds the golden gate.
We spin and sway, we laugh and cry,
In this carousel, we always try.

With every loop, we learn to dance,
Taking a leap, we seize the chance.
From silly starts to heartfelt ends,
In cycles, we connect with friends.

The Dance of Doubt and Discovery

Doubt flirts like a clumsy clown,
Stumbling in a floppy gown.
Discovery wears a dapper hat,
Whirling round like a curious cat.

They tango through the twists of fate,
Chasing answers, oh so great.
But questions pop like bubblegum,
With every snap, new thoughts come numb.

In this crazy, silly waltz,
We trip and tumble, blame the faults.
Yet through the chaos, smiles arise,
As we find truth in each surprise.

So let us dance, oh what a sight,
Laughing through the sleepless night.
Doubt and discovery, side by side,
In this wacky world, we take a ride.

Reflections on a Wandering Path

Wandering down this winding trail,
With a map that's full of fail.
Turns that lead to nowhere fast,
Yet we giggle as we pass.

Mirrors flaunt our funny faces,
In these unexpected places.
Searching for clues in every crack,
While the universe gives us a whack.

Each step brings a new small jest,
Are we lost or simply blessed?
With every stumble, laughter grows,
As the silly wind gently blows.

Let's embrace this wobbly quest,
With giggles, we feel our best.
In reflections of our quirky fate,
We find joy—why hesitate?

A Journey Through Paradoxes

Why do we chase what we can't grasp?
Is it profit or just a silly gasp?
The snail moves slow, but the rabbit's in fright,
Both end up lost in the dead of night.

We laugh at fate while it takes its toll,
Juggling dreams like a circus role.
Is the key to know it's a cosmic joke?
Or maybe just mirrors and words that provoke?

Life's a riddle, a puzzle to box,
Is it chance, or are we just laughing at rocks?
As we tangle our feet in the shoelaces tight,
We trip and we roll, oh what a delight!

In the end, is it wisdom or in jest?
Counting our blessings while failing the test.
With a wink and a nod, we carry the load,
Enjoy the ride on this curious road.

Unwritten Narratives

Pen in hand, the story begins,
Plot twists that lead to multiple spins.
A hero trips over their own two feet,
While villains order takeout to eat.

Page by page, we scribble and laugh,
Dancing on lines like it's a photograph.
Each plot twist is just us playing pretend,
As we fumble through pages and hope for a friend.

Chasing the words like a cat with its tail,
Skipping through chapters that are bound to derail.
In the margins, we doodle our dreams,
Whether they're silly or bursting at the seams.

Every blank space a chance for a punch,
Finding the joy in a comical crunch.
As the author, we take the grand lead,
In a tale that's absurd, but oh so agreed!

Beneath the Surface

Diving deep where the fishies play,
Waving at bubbles, come out to say.
Is that wisdom or just some old shoe?
Underneath waves, it's all askew.

We paddle in circles, splash here and there,
Fishy conspiracies float in the air.
Chasing shadows where light won't abide,
Hoping for answers we playfully hide.

Questions like seaweed wrap tight around,
Each strand a mystery, never quite found.
Are we just swimmers in someone's soup?
Or marionettes in a jolly old troop?

By the tide, we laugh at our quest,
As capricious thoughts jostle and jest.
Under the surface, we find what we crave,
A salute to the odd, a chorus so brave.

Fables of the Human Heart

Once upon a time in a land of pretend,
Where giggles and sighs would always blend.
Hearts dressed in armor, charging with zest,
Turned out to be a ridiculous quest.

A dragon of doubt took a seat for a chat,
While a mouse with a hat claimed it's all just flat.
They plotted together a tale full of cheer,
With punchlines that echoed and knocked on the year.

Every giggle a chapter, each tear a verse,
Adventures unfold, some truly perverse.
In the end, what's real, what's simply a bluff?
Life's but a fable, and it's certainly tough!

So here's to the stories that make us all laugh,
In the drama of living, we write our own path.
With twists and with quirks, our hearts sing along,
In the epic of life, we're the heroes of song.

Beneath the Stars

Under the blanket night, we lie,
Wondering why the clouds float by.
Is the moon just a giant cheese?
Or did aliens plant those trees?

Laughter echoes, we share a jest,
What if life's a cosmic quest?
Twirling with planets, dancing with fate,
Maybe the meaning's up for debate.

Shooting stars wink and they tease,
"Find your truth, if you please!"
With a giggle and a snort, we play,
Chasing mysteries that lead us astray.

So, let's toast to the stars above,
In this galaxy, let's spread some love.
Life's a riddle, or a game,
And we're all just playing for fame.

Within the Heart

Deep in the chest, a beat goes thump,
Is it joy, or just a grump?
Squirrels gather with nuts so bold,
They seem to know what life has told.

Pumping passion, or maybe lunch?
Is it love, or just a hunch?
Hearts tangled like spaghetti strands,
Or are they just shifting sands?

So many feelings piled in a sack,
Like a jester with a silly knack.
With each thud, we march in glee,
Perhaps, it's just on DVD.

Dancing rhythms deep within,
Is it chaos or a win?
In this maze, we twirl and spin,
With heartbeats that always grin.

Ethereal Musings

Floating thoughts in a cloud of dreams,
Ideas shine, or so it seems.
Are we whispers in the air?
Or just dust bunnies without a care?

Questions flutter like butterflies,
Wings of colors, oh what a surprise!
Do the answers hide in plain sight?
Or are we just wandering in twilight?

Through the fog of our own delight,
Chasing shadows in the night.
With a wink and a cosmic giggle,
We twirl through life, and then we wiggle.

So let's ponder, let's be absurd,
In this mystery yet undeterred.
Ethereal musings, nonsensically bright,
We'll laugh and dance till dawn's first light.

The Canvas of Thought

Brushstrokes fly on the canvas vast,
Splashing ideas, a colorful blast.
Is life a painting, or a scribble on chart?
Every shade reflects the human heart?

The reds are laughter, the blues are sighs,
Swirls of confusion, brightening skies.
With every stroke, a journey begins,
A messy masterpiece where no one wins.

We dip our brushes in whimsy and glee,
Creating art that's wild and free.
Oh, what a sight, this colorful life,
A palette of joy wrapped in strife!

So let's paint wildly, with zest and cheer,
Every drop of color, a strand clever.
On this canvas, let's create our lore,
A funny tale, forever more.

Echoes in Eternity

In the halls where echoes play,
Life's punchlines bounce, come what may.
Is it wisdom, or silly chime?
Perhaps it's just a dance in time?

Whispers of moments flutter and sway,
Like butterflies lost on their way.
Can laughter survive the hands of fate?
Or does it just fold and wait?

Time ticks on, with giggles galore,
Collecting memories, asking for more.
In eternity's grip, we chase our tales,
Amidst the zany wind that never fails.

So here we stand, in this timeless spree,
Eternal echoes, a funny decree.
Let's embrace the giggles, the blissful strife,
After all, what's better than this jolly life?

Mirrors of the Soul

In a funhouse, I stare wide-eyed,
Reflections blur, oh what a ride!
Laughter echoes, as I twist and spin,
Searching for depth where the chaos begins.

My nose is huge, my hair a mess,
Is that really me? I must confess!
I ponder deeply, yet giggle still,
Life's just a game, so what's the thrill?

I trip on thoughts while chasing dreams,
The mirror laughs, or so it seems.
If truth is bold, then let it be,
A comedy show starring me!

With each new glance, I learn to jest,
In this circus, I do my best.
So here's a toast to all the flaws,
In life's goofy mirror, we'll find the cause.

Chords of Connection

Strumming strings on a sunny day,
Making music in a silly way.
The notes dance wildly, in the air,
Life's a jam session that we all share.

Tune your heart, let laughter flow,
Mixed up harmonies, steal the show!
A melody born from playful strife,
Each quirky chord, a slice of life.

Misplays happen, but that's the fun,
Life's a song that's never done.
So grab your friends, let's make a sound,
In this wacky world, joy is found.

Together we laugh, together we sing,
In the orchestra of everything!
So turn it up, let the world know,
Life's just a gig, and we're the show!

Rivers of Reflection

I dipped my toes in thoughts today,
The river laughed, 'Come splash and play!'
Waves of whimsy, current of glee,
What's deeper than shallow? Come see!

Floating past worries with a grin,
I thought I lost, but where to begin?
Ripples carry secrets, oh what a ride,
In this murky water, I can't hide.

Silly fish swim beneath the waves,
With wisdom tucked in watery caves.
They giggle and tease, but what do they know?
In this river of life, just let it flow!

So paddle along in this quirky spree,
Let laughter echo, just be free!
For in every splash and splashy knock,
Life's a river; we're on the clock!

Tapestry of Trials

In threads of laughter, we stitch all day,
Mismatched patterns in a funny way.
Each knot a story, each twist a laugh,
Life's tapestry folds, oh what a craft!

Sewing up blunders with glitter and cheer,
Every mishap is bright and clear.
With needle and thread, we dance through strife,
Creating a quilt that's called 'Our Life'.

Bright colors clash in this fabric's tale,
Stitches of joy that never pale.
In each fabric piece, a memory's spun,
Life's just a blanket, oh what fun!

So let's weave together through laughter and tears,
Embracing the chaos across the years.
For in this tapestry, there's room for all,
An artful existence where we'll never fall!

The Whisper of Tomorrow

I asked my socks for wisdom,
They just laughed and ran away.
A squirrel gave me a riddle,
But I forgot it yesterday.

The stars seem to be texting,
Yet I don't have their number.
I tried to crack the code,
Now I'm lost in a slumber.

Balloons float with no agenda,
Chasing dreams like they're dogs.
A fish wears a tiny hat,
And debates with the logs.

Each laugh is a secret,
Wrapped in bright paper and cheer.
I'll search for the answers,
With a bucket of ice cream near.

Notes from the Cosmos

I wrote a note to the universe,
It bounced back with a sneeze.
A comet threw confetti,
While I tripped over the breeze.

Aliens watch me dancing,
From their shiny UFO.
I offered them a donut,
They preferred Jell-O, you know?

The moon is a huge cookie,
But I can't reach it tonight.
I'll settle for the starlight,
And a couch that feels just right.

Galaxies spin in laughter,
Twirling in a cosmic play.
I'll join their wild waltz,
And forget the light of day.

Fragmented Realities

I've lost my marbles again,
They rolled under the couch.
I asked a lamp for guidance,
But it just gave a slouch.

Mirrors reflect my chaos,
Smiling back in delight.
Do I wave or do I frown?
It's a puzzling sight.

In the fridge, I found my dreams,
Chilling next to the peas.
They whispered of adventures,
While hiding from the cheese.

With mismatched socks for wisdom,
And cereal box insights,
I'll puzzle through this madness,
Dancing with my breakfast bites.

Within the Storm of Questions

I've got a storm of questions,
Raining down like wet socks.
A frog in a top hat listens,
And checks his fancy clocks.

Is the toaster really wise?
Or just good at browning bread?
My cat thinks he's the answer,
But he just wants my bed.

I wandered into a pickle,
And found a worm with a map.
It said, 'Life's a big adventure,'
Then took a nap on my lap.

The squirrels are the philosophers,
Debating where to bury nuts.
I'll join their round table now,
Because laughter, that's a must.

Dreams on the Edge

I dreamt of cheese, a mountain so vast,
But when I climbed, it crumbled too fast.
I wore my socks, all mismatched and bright,
Chasing my cat in the pale moonlight.

I searched for treasure under my bed,
Found only gum and a doll's little head.
With each crazy thought, I scribble and draw,
What if life's just a cosmic big flaw?

Pancakes in space, floating fluffy and round,
Would syrup be gravity or just stick to the ground?
With laughter and giggles, we dance on this thread,
Perhaps it's a joke that we all haven't read.

In dreams we buffet, life's quirky buffet,
Here's to a banquet of humor today!
Live with a smile, like a balloon in the breeze,
Maybe the secret's just being a tease.

Reflections in the Abyss

I stared in the mirror, who's that smiling back?
Is it me or a potato with too much smack?
In the darkness, I ponder, with a tinge of dread,
Does my brain have a glitch? Or just need some bread?

The cat gives advice; it's always profound,
'Just nap and eat fish, avoid what's around.'
But what if the fish has a secret to share?
Do I risk losing sleep for a tale of despair?

Each thought's an echo, boomerang of fun,
My fears in the shadows, they all play and run.
Like socks in the dryer, they twist and they spin,
Is it me or the universe playing violin?

I twirl in the chaos, a dance of absurd,
With a wink at the void, I'm utterly stirred.
Life's just a riddle, but I laugh with glee,
Perhaps it's all silly—what will be, will be!

Navigating the Unknown

In a boat made of dreams, I sail with a grin,
With oars made of laughter, let the chaos begin.
The map's upside down and the compass is broke,
I ask for directions from a talking oak.

The stars play hide and seek, oh what a chase,
One's a dancing jellybean, full of grace.
"Where to?" I ask, but they all disappear,
I guess I'll just follow the smell of fried beer.

I bumble through jungles of ideas that clash,
Tripping on thoughts, in a frantic mad dash.
But at every wrong turn, I stumble on gold,
Like finding lost socks, their stories untold.

So here's to adventures, both twisted and wild,
Through mazes of oddness, I remain the child.
With a laugh and a grin, it's joy that I seek,
The unknown is silly, it goes bonkers each week!

Signs in the Silence

In the hush of the night, where the whispers reside,
I read the tea leaves; they giggle and slide.
"Is life just a riddle?" I ponder and wait,
But all that I get is a shrug from my plate.

The clock sings a tune, but it's stuck on rewind,
Ticking away at thoughts that are perfectly blind.
A dandelion's wish floats up with a whirl,
It laughs as it drifts, like a carefree girl.

Each shadow a sign, a message unclear,
"Maybe just dance," suggests the full beer.
But what if the answers are hidden in jest?
I'll wear my clown shoes and laugh with the rest.

So let's toast to the awkward, the weird, and the fun,
In the silence of night, our shenanigans run.
Life's a comedy show, each moment a chance,
To chuckle, to wiggle, to twirl in a dance!

Uncharted Realms of Thought

In a world where socks get lost,
And cereal's a breakfast cost,
I ponder why the moon's so bright,
While dancing with my cat at night.

Pizza slices, oh what a dream,
With extra cheese, I softly scream,
Are we just bubbles in a bath?
Or cosmic jokes of cosmic math?

What if penguins wore bow ties?
Or fish rode bikes beneath blue skies?
I sip my drink, confusion grows,
As answers dance on my big toes.

With laughter echoing through my brain,
I search for sense in sheer mundane,
Yet like a clown, I swerve and bend,
This quest for truth may never end!

Reflections in Still Waters

I looked in water, what a sight,
A raccoon wearing sneakers bright,
It shrugged, as if to say, 'Dear friend,
Life's a puzzle, no clear end.'

A rubber ducky floats nearby,
Quacking wisdom, oh so spry,
He quips, 'Why worry? Just be bold,
Embrace the weird, be uncontrolled!'

A fish, with glasses, reads the news,
While frogs in togas dance with blues,
They croak, 'Dig deep, don't take a pause,
Laugh at the chaos, it's the cause!'

So I toss crumbs, watch ripples form,
In this still pond, such wacky norm,
I shout, 'I'm lost!' then grin with glee,
For fun's the point, and that's the key!

Echoes in the Void

In a quiet room, a sock sings loud,
Toasting toast that's very proud,
I wonder if my fridge has dreams,
Of tangled wires and crazy schemes.

The clock ticks jokes, the walls reply,
As pillows whisper, 'Oh my, oh my!'
A thought escapes, it bounces back,
Like rubber balls on a snack attack.

What's life, you ask? A riddle spied,
In every crumb and crumbly ride,
The echo laughs, it knows the score,
Just breathe and munch—who could want more?

So here I sit, absurd and free,
With thoughts as wiggly as spaghetti,
In voids we find what's most absurd,
A symphony of laughter heard!

Mosaic of Moments

Each day's a tile, a bit askew,
With splashes bright in every hue,
Coffee spills and laughter flows,
As goofy thoughts bring smiles, who knows?

My dog's a poet in disguise,
With tales of squirrels and great surprise,
Who knew a bark could hold such weight?
In every woof, a twist of fate.

I wear my pants inside-out today,
It's fashion week, they all must say,
As I dance like nobody can see,
Life's silly moments are key to glee.

So join this dance of odd delight,
And find the joy in every slight,
For in this quilt, we laugh and strive,
It's chaos here, but we're alive!

Beyond the Horizon

Chasing clues in the bright blue sky,
Finding answers as kites swoop and fly.
The sun's got a joke, I laugh till I cry,
Maybe we're just dots, and life's one big pie.

Puzzles and riddles dance in my head,
Like socks without partners, where have they fled?
I trip over thoughts, fall out of my bed,
Do fish think about oceans? Or just break bread?

Each day's a ticket on this crazy ride,
Where I'm the passenger, with pizza as my guide.
If wisdom is gold, then I've surely pried,
A world full of giggles, can't be denied!

So here's to the quirks and the bumps on the street,
To laughter and mischief, a life that's a treat.
With questions like candy, both sour and sweet,
We keep dancing circles, on our own two feet.

In Search of Illumination.

With a flashlight in hand, I'll explore the night,
Stumbling on mysteries that spark my delight.
Why do the stars giggle? Is it sheer fright?
Or just because meteors are too fast to bite?

I tripped on a thought, landed in a dream,
Chasing after answers, or so it may seem.
Why's life like a movie, but with no theme?
Maybe it's comedy – or so my friends beam.

The clock ticks slowly, while I run in place,
Wearing mismatched socks in this peculiar race.
Life's a circus act, full of laughs to embrace,
And all I can do is smile, just in case.

In search of the spark that keeps us alive,
We juggle our doubts, oh how we strive.
With humor as fuel, we dance and we jive,
Turning frowns into giggles, as we all thrive.

Questions in the Quiet

In the hush of the night, I ponder and peek,
Why do owls hoot secrets, yet never speak?
Are clouds just cotton, or do they sneak?
And do chairs ever wonder who's taking a seat?

Whispers of doubt float like breeze through the air,
As I spin in my thoughts, what's really so rare?
Perhaps I'm just hungry for thoughts that are fair,
While my brain's like a circus, a real wild affair!

A moment of stillness, what will I unearth?
Is laughter a fruit of this quirky old Earth?
With questions like jellybeans, packed with mirth,
We ponder and giggle, all cherishing the worth.

Amidst all the puzzles, let's relish the ride,
Adventure awaits, come take a side.
With humor as our guide, no need to hide,
We'll dance through the chaos, our joy amplified.

Whispers of Existence

What's hiding behind that leaf in the breeze?
Is it a small elf trying to tease?
Or a squirrel on a mission, with nuts as his keys?
Oh, laughter flows freely like laughter from trees.

In shadows of moments, my mind starts to play,
Why do cats always sleep throughout the whole day?
Are they dreaming of fish, or just shades of gray?
As I hunt for the truth, I try to obey.

With chuckles as buddies and smiles to spare,
Let's unwrap the gifts that float in the air.
Curiosity's a joker, with tangled hair,
In this comedy of life, we're the stars of our fair!

So let the whispers tickle your thoughts as they roam,
In silliness found, can we call this home?
With joy as our anchor, we'll proudly comb,
Through the questions of existence — let's happily roam!

Chasing Horizons

We run to the edge, where the sky meets the ground,
With ice cream in hand, our thoughts spinning round.
Questions like pinwheels, they twist and they twirl,
Caught in a whirlwind, we dance and we swirl.

Like cats in a box, we ponder our fate,
Each meow is a riddle that makes us feel great.
We chuckle at logic, it rarely aligns,
Yet here we are laughing in plenty of signs.

A squirrel on a branch shares secrets of cheer,
It claims there's a prize if we don't live in fear.
With shiny distractions, we sip on our dreams,
Unraveling puzzles like puzzles of creams.

So what if the path is a jigsaw of laughs?
We wear mismatched socks and ignore the gaffs.
Through giggles and chaos, we'll find our way free,
With tickles and giggles, just let it be me!

Illusions of Certainty

We build our own castles with clouds made of fluff,
Declaring with confidence, but is that enough?
Winking at fortune, we shuffle our feet,
Life's like a dance where we stumble and greet.

Like fortune cookies giggling in a drawer,
We crack them for wisdom, and then laugh some more.
An owl with a monocle, struts through the night,
Sipping on answers that dart out of sight.

Juggling misgivings as we skip through the grass,
Try not to trip over the thoughts that we pass.
As logic does cartwheels, we shake our minds free,
With laughter as currency, we float like a bee.

What if certainty's just a hat that we wear,
That comes with a tag saying "Handle with care"?
Let's toss it in jest, like a coin into air,
Laughing at notions that fade into rare.

Tethered to Wonder

We're tied to our whims like balloons in a breeze,
Never quite knowing which way they will tease.
With curious minds, like kittens at play,
We chase after answers that sneak far away.

Wobbling thoughts, like jelly on a plate,
Bouncing around as we ponder our fate.
With googly eyes, we observe with delight,
The mysteries swirling in day and in night.

Giraffes in tuxedos hold councils at noon,
Discussing the merits of dancing to tune.
Could marshmallows guide us on paths we can't see?
Or is that just nonsense; can it really be free?

As we tether our dreams to the stars up above,
We laugh at the cosmic embrace of our love.
In a world full of wonders, we giggle and sway,
Life's just a game that we play day by day.

Beneath the Surface

Beneath all the chatter, there's silence and quirk,
Like squirrels in a suit, going quite berserk.
We paddle through puddles, splashing in jest,
With rubber duck wisdom, that put us to test.

Tickle monsters lurking in each passing thought,
We question the things we once knew, but forgot.
In the slapstick of life, we slip and we slide,
Hilarity reigns when we can't run and hide.

With spoons made of candy, we stir up our fate,
While sipping on laughter, we contemplate weight.
There's depth in the giggles, it's wild and it's rare,
For life's just a party, no need for despair.

So dive down the rabbit hole, bring rubbery cheer,
For every misstep holds laughter so near.
Let's unravel the puzzles, paint dreams with a grin,
We're dancing on surfaces; the fun's where we begin!

www.ingramcontent.com/pod-product-compliance
Lightning Source LLC
Chambersburg PA
CBHW072218070526
44585CB00015B/1386